Kylie Jean
BREAKFAST
Recipe Queen

by Gail Green
and Marci Peschke

PICTURE WINDOW BOOKS
a capstone imprint

Kylie Jean is published by Picture Window Books
A Capstone Imprint
1710 Roe Crest Drive
North Mankato, Minnesota 56003
www.mycapstone.com

Library of Congress Cataloging-in-Publication Data
Cataloging-in-Publication information is on file with the Library of Congress.
Names: Green, Gail, and Marci Peschke, authors. | Mourning, Tuesday, illustrator.
ISBN 978-1-5158-2850-1 (library binding)
ISBN 978-1-5158-2854-9 (paperback)
ISBN 978-1-5158-2858-7 (eBook PDF)

Editor: Mari Bolte
Designer: Tracy McCabe
Production Specialist: Kris Wilfahrt

Photo Credits:
All recipe photos by Capstone Studio/Karon Dubke
Design elements: Shutterstock

Printed and bound in the United States of America.
PA021

TABLE OF CONTENTS

Hey y'all, rise and shine and grab your skillet, because we're making breakfast!

I love pancakes, and my GRIDDLE DIPPERS have chocolate chips, bacon, and pecans. When I hear someone say MAPLE SYRUP, I say YUM! This book will give you cooking tips and step-by-step directions to make breakfast for your whole family. I'm going to make the HEARTY BREAKFAST PIZZA for T.J. and UGLY BROTHER'S SWEET BREATH BAGELS for my favorite pup. Momma will love the RISE AND SHINE SMOOTHIES. I might even make one for her on Mother's Day. BREAKFAST IS THE FIRST AND MOST IMPORTANT MEAL OF THE DAY, SO BE SURE TO PICK A *yummy recipe!*

CONVERSIONS

1/4 teaspoon	1.25 grams or milliliters
1/2 teaspoon	2.5 g or mL
1 teaspoon	5 g or mL
1 tablespoon	15 g or mL
1/4 cup	57 g (dry) or 60 mL (liquid)
1/3 cup	75 g (dry) or 80 mL (liquid)
1/2 cup	114 g (dry) or 125 mL (liquid)
2/3 cup	150 g (dry) or 160 mL (liquid)
3/4 cup	170 g (dry) or 175 mL (liquid)
1 cup	227 g (dry) or 240 mL (liquid)
1 quart	950 mL

Fahrenheit (°F)	Celsius (°C)
325°	160°
350°	180°
375°	190°
400°	200°
425°	220°
450°	230°

This pancake in a pan is a delicious fall breakfast treat, but you can make them any ol' time you want. Be extra careful when chopping the apples! I like to save the cores for Ugly Brother.

OOEY, GOOEY OVEN PANCAKE

BATTER:
½ cup milk
½ cup flour
3 eggs, beaten
1 teaspoon cinnamon
1 tablespoon sugar
1 pinch of salt

APPLE MIXTURE:
1 large apple, peeled and chopped
1 teaspoon lemon juice
1 teaspoon cinnamon
1 teaspoon sugar
2 tablespoons butter

TOPPING:
1 tablespoon lemon juice
2 tablespoons melted butter
2 teaspoons cinnamon
½ cup brown sugar

SPECIAL TOOLS:
9-inch (22.8 centimeter) cake pan
cooking spray
electric mixer
basting or pastry brush

INSTRUCTIONS:

1. Reposition an oven rack to the bottom slot. Ask an adult to preheat oven to 450 degrees. Spray the cake pan with cooking spray and set it in the oven.

2. Combine the milk, flour, eggs, cinnamon, sugar, and salt in a mixing bowl. With an adult's help, beat with an electric mixer on low until well mixed but slightly lumpy.

3. Have an adult to warm a frying pan over low heat. Add the apple mixture. Sauté the apples until tender.

4. Ask an adult to remove the cake pan from the oven. Spoon the apples into the pan. Pour the batter over the apples. Then return the pan to the oven.

5. Bake for 10 to 12 minutes, or until the batter puffs up. Reduce heat to 350 degrees and bake an additional 10 minutes or until golden brown.

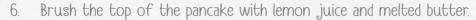

6. Brush the top of the pancake with lemon juice and melted butter.

7. Mix the cinnamon and brown sugar together. Sprinkle it over the pancake. Have an adult return the pan to the oven and bake an additional 5 minutes until topping is melted and gooey.

8. With an adult's help, remove the pancake from the oven. Serve immediately.

CREATIVE OPTION:
You can also bake this in a 9-inch cast-iron skillet. If you don't like apples, try other fruits such as sliced peaches, halved strawberries, or whole blueberries. Or add fresh fruit to a plain pancake before you sprinkle on the topping.

TIP:
The type of apple used will determine how sweet the pancake will be. Choose a Honeycrisp for a super sweet pancake or a Granny Smith for a tart flavor.

My daddy likes to help make this breakfast treat, but he likes to eat them even more! These Griddle Dippers have two of his favorite ingredients — chocolate and bacon. Yum!

GRIDDLE DIPPERS
WITH CRUNCHY PECAN MAPLE DIPPING SYRUP

INGREDIENTS:
1 cup flour

2 teaspoons baking powder

½ teaspoon baking soda

1 ½ tablespoons brown sugar

¼ teaspoon salt

1 egg

3 tablespoons buttermilk

2 tablespoons butter, room temperature

2 egg whites

2 tablespoons granulated sugar

zest from an orange,
about 2 to 3 tablespoons

¾ cup semi—sweet chocolate chips

8 to 10 bacon strips, cooked and drained

SPECIAL TOOLS:
griddle

electric mixer

squeeze bottle

INSTRUCTIONS:

1. Ask an adult to preheat the griddle to 375 degrees, or medium—high heat.

2. Combine flour, baking powder, baking soda, brown sugar, and salt in a mixing bowl. Stir together and set aside.

3. Place egg, buttermilk, and butter in a small bowl. Mix well.

4. Pour egg whites into another mixing bowl. Use clean beaters and, with an adult's help, whip on high until frothy. Add the granulated sugar and beat until peaks begin to form.

5. Fold the butter mixture into the dry mixture until combined. Stir in the orange zest and chocolate chips. Gently fold in the whipped egg whites.

6. Pour half the batter into a squeeze bottle.

7. Ask an adult to preheat a large griddle on medium—high heat. When hot, grease with butter.

8. Squeeze some of the batter onto the hot griddle in a long oval shape. It should be a little longer and wider than a bacon strip. Place a strip of bacon in the center of the batter and press lightly. Add more batter on top in a wavy, squiggly pattern.

9. Reduce heat to medium. Cook 3 to 4 minutes, until large bubbles form on the surface of the pancake.

10. Using a spatula, carefully flip the pancake and continue to cook for 2 to 3 minutes.

11. Remove the cooked pancake from the griddle and place on warming plate. Cover with foil and store in a low temperature oven until all the pancakes have been cooked.

12. Add more butter to the griddle. Repeat steps 8 through 11, refilling the squeeze bottle with the remaining batter as needed.

13. Serve with Crunchy Pecan Maple Dipping Syrup.

TIP:
Have an adult separate the egg whites from the egg yolks. If there is even a little yolk in the whites — or your bowl or beaters aren't clean — they won't whip.

Make sure the hole at the tip of the squeeze bottle is large enough for the batter to easily flow out. Cut the tip larger if needed.

CREATIVE OPTION:
If you don't have buttermilk, use plain yogurt or sour cream instead.

To save on time, used packaged pancake mix and add orange zest.

CRUNCHY PECAN MAPLE DIPPING SYRUP:

INGREDIENTS:
1 cup water
2 cups sugar
½ cup finely chopped pecans
1 teaspoon maple extract
4 tablespoons butter

SPECIAL TOOLS:
wide mouth mason jar

INSTRUCTIONS:
1. Mix water and sugar in a saucepan. With an adult's help, cook over medium heat, stirring continually until sugar is dissolved.
2. Reduce heat to low as soon as the mixture comes to a boil. Stir in pecans. Reduce heat and simmer for 5 minutes.
3. Remove from heat. Stir in maple extract and butter.
4. Let sit for 15 to 20 minutes so the syrup can fully absorb the pecan flavor.
5. Pour the syrup into a wide mouth mason jar for easy pancake dipping.

In the summer, we pick blueberries at Nanny and Pa's Lickskillet Farm. They make the perfect blender breakfast! Choose your favorite fruits for these colorful coolers.

RISE AND SHINE SMOOTHIES

STRAWBERRY BANANA
INGREDIENTS:
¾ cup fresh or frozen strawberries
1 banana, frozen
½ cup ice
1 cup milk

PAPAY-NEAPPLE
INGREDIENTS:
½ cup fresh or frozen papaya
¼ cup fresh pineapple
¼ cup coconut water
½ teaspoon coconut extract
½ cup ice

BLUEBERRY KIWI
INGREDIENTS:
½ cup frozen blueberries
¼ cup fresh kiwi, peeled
1 cup yogurt

MANGO-BERRY
INGREDIENTS:
½ cup fresh or frozen mango
¼ cup fresh or frozen raspberries
½ cup orange juice

SPECIAL TOOLS:
blender

INSTRUCTIONS:

1. Place the strawberries, banana, ice, and milk in a blender. Have an adult blend everything for 1 minute until smooth. Pour into a glass and place in the refrigerator or freezer. Rinse out the blender.

2. Repeat step 1, but with blueberries, kiwi, and yogurt.

3. Repeat step 1, but with papaya, pineapple, coconut water, coconut extract, and ice.

4. Repeat step 1, but with mango, raspberries, and orange juice.

5. Skewer leftover fruit pieces on a toothpick. Decorate the smoothies with toothpicks before serving.

CREATIVE OPTION:
Make every smoothie dairy free by replacing milk or yogurt with one banana and ½ cup crushed ice. Add a teaspoon of vanilla, coconut, almond, or orange extract.

TIP:
Give your smoothies a boost! Add nuts or nut butter, oats, flax, unsweetened coconut or coconut oil, chia seeds, matcha tea, or ginger. You can also add vegetables, such as avocado, carrots, beets, spinach, or kale.

These colorful waffles remind me of my best cousin, Lucy.
She loves sparkles, sprinkles, rainbows, and unicorns. I like to use
the leftovers to make ice-cream sandwiches. Sprinkles on mine, please!

RAINBOW WAFFLES

INGREDIENTS:

2 jumbo eggs
1/3 cup vegetable oil
1 tablespoon vanilla extract
1 2/3 cup buttermilk
2 cups flour
3 tablespoons sugar

4 teaspoons baking powder
pinch of salt
gel food coloring in four colors

SPECIAL TOOLS:
squeeze bottles or piping bags
waffle iron
cooking spray

INSTRUCTIONS:

1. Whisk the eggs, oil, vanilla, and buttermilk together in a small bowl until frothy. Set aside.

2. Mix flour, sugar, and baking powder together in a separate, larger bowl.

3. Gradually stir the egg mixture into the dry ingredients, blending into a lumpy batter. Do not overmix.

4. Divide the batter equally into four small bowls. Add a few drops of food coloring to each bowl and mix well. Add additional food coloring, one drop at a time, until you get the color you like.

5. Spoon each color batter into a different squeeze bottle or piping bag.

6. Ask an adult to heat the waffle iron. Spray both sides of the waffle iron with cooking spray.

7. Squeeze waffle batter colors onto the base of the waffle iron in strips, squiggles, or circles.

8. Close the waffle iron top. With an adult's help, cook according to the waffle iron's instructions.

9. Have the adult remove each waffle immediately after cooking. Repeat the process for each waffle.

10. Top with whipped cream, vanilla yogurt, fresh fruit, or chopped nuts.

CREATIVE OPTION:
For a marbled look, use a toothpick to swirl the batter on the waffle iron.

TIP:
Instead of squeezing the batter onto the waffle iron, you can spoon it directly from the individual bowls. Or you can make a piping bag with zip-top bags. Spoon the batter into the bags. Then add food coloring and roll the bag in your hands until the color is mixed. Cut a small opening in one corner to squeeze out the batter.

Nothing says Texas like tacos, and these Cheesy Egg Taco Bowls are the best way to start out the morning in Jacksonville. T.J. and Daddy like to see who can build the biggest bowl!

CHEESY EGG TACO BOWL

INGREDIENTS:

4 burrito-sized flour tortillas
olive oil
¼ cup red bell pepper, diced
clove of fresh garlic
(or ½ teaspoon minced)
6 eggs
¾ cup shredded cheddar cheese

avocado, diced
black olives, sliced
2 tablespoons cilantro, chopped
salsa or hot sauce

SPECIAL TOOLS:

four oven-safe coffee mugs
basting or pastry brush

INSTRUCTIONS:

1. Set the mugs on a baking sheet. Ask an adult to preheat oven to 400 degrees.

2. Microwave one tortilla for 12 to 15 seconds. Brush olive oil generously on both sides. Drape the tortilla over a mug.

3. Repeat step 2 for remaining tortillas and mugs. Bake for 8 to 10 minutes or until crispy, slightly puffed, and golden brown.

4. Have an adult remove the tortillas from the oven. Cool 7 to 10 minutes before carefully removing from the cups.

5. With an adult's help, add a tablespoon of oil to a frying pan, and turn the burner to medium heat. Sauté the red pepper and garlic for 2 to 3 minutes.

6. Whisk the eggs in a small mixing bowl and add them to the pan. Scramble until the eggs are set.

7. Divide the egg mixture into the four taco bowls. Top with cheese, avocado, olives, and cilantro.

8. Spoon salsa or hot sauce over the top, according to taste. Add a cilantro sprig for garnish.

CREATIVE OPTION:

Use taco-sized tortillas and a 12-section muffin tin to create mini taco bowls or cups. Turn the muffin tin upside down. Coat with cooking spray. Then place tortillas in the space between four muffin sections. Bake at 375 degrees for 8 to 10 minutes.

TIP:

Add additional ingredients to the taco bowls, such as refried beans, cooked black beans, cooked sweet corn kernels, diced and cooked sweet potatoes, or diced tomatoes.

Sometimes I wake up late and nearly miss the bus. I don't like to keep my favorite bus driver, Mr. Jim, waiting. These healthy energy bars make a great breakfast when you're running late!

GRAB 'N' GO ENERGY BARS

INGREDIENTS:

2 cups rolled oats

½ cup sliced almonds, chopped pecans, or walnuts

⅓ cup pumpkin or sunflower seeds

2 tablespoons honey

¼ cup maple syrup

1 cup nut butter (such as peanut butter or almond butter)

1 teaspoon vanilla or almond extract

1 teaspoon cinnamon

½ cup unsweetened shredded coconut

⅓ cup cherry chips

SPECIAL TOOLS:

8-inch (20.3-cm) square cake pan

parchment paper

INSTRUCTIONS:

1. Ask an adult to preheat oven to 350 degrees.

2. Combine oats, nuts, and seeds in mixing bowl. Spread the mixture on a baking sheet. With an adult's help, toast in the oven for 10 to 12 minutes or until slightly golden. Then ask the adult to remove the baking sheet from the oven. Let everything cool, and return the mixture to the mixing bowl.

3. Place the honey, maple syrup, and nut butter in a small saucepan. With an adult's help, stir over low heat until well blended. Remove from heat. Mix in extract. Let cool slightly.

4. Spoon the nut butter mixture into the mixing bowl. Add remaining ingredients. Mix thoroughly until well blended and smooth.

5. Line the baking pan with parchment paper. Make sure the paper also covers the sides of the pan and hangs over the edges.

6. Spread the mixture evenly into the pan. Be sure to press it firmly into the corners and sides.

7. Place the pan in the freezer for 30 minutes or until set.

8. Remove the mixture from the pan by lifting the parchment paper. Then set it on a cutting board. Ask an adult to cut into bars.

9. Wrap and refrigerate or freeze the individual bars in a sealed, airtight freezer bag or container.

TIP:
For a nut-free version, omit nuts and increase seed mixture to 2/3 cup. Use soy or sunflower seed butter instead of nut butter, and eliminate the coconut.

CREATIVE OPTION:
Make a dipped bar! Before wrapping, dip your bar in Crunchy Maple Pecan Dipping Syrup. Then roll in coconut, chocolate chips, or finely chopped nuts.

My big brother, T.J., would eat pizza for every meal. And now he can with this hearty breakfast pizza! I bet he'll eat more than one slice.

HEARTY BREAKFAST PIZZA WITH HASH BROWN CRUST

INGREDIENTS:

2 cups frozen shredded hash brown potatoes, thawed

1 cup shredded cheese

2 tablespoons cooking oil

3 garlic cloves, minced

½ cup green onions, diced

⅓ cup red bell pepper, cut into strips

¼ cup mushrooms, sliced

½ cup tomatoes, sliced

1 ½ cups fresh baby spinach

4 eggs

¼ cup milk

salt and pepper to taste

⅓ cup bacon, cooked, drained, and crumbled

4 sausage links, cooked and sliced

SPECIAL TOOLS:

9-inch (22.8 cm) pie pan

cooking spray

INSTRUCTIONS:

1. Ask an adult to preheat oven to 375 degrees.

2. Coat the pie pan with cooking spray.

3. Press hash brown potatoes into the pie pan. Bake for 9 to 10 minutes. Have an adult remove the pie pan from the oven. Sprinkle half the shredded cheese on top. Set aside.

4. With an adult's help, pour oil into a skillet, and turn the burner to medium-high. Add garlic, green onions, and pepper strips. Sauté for 30 seconds. Add mushrooms and tomatoes. Cook an additional 30 seconds. Mix in the spinach and cook for 2 to 3 minutes or until wilted.

5. Spread the sautéed vegetables over the hash brown crust.

6. Whisk eggs, milk, salt, and pepper in a bowl until well mixed.

7. Pour egg mixture over the vegetable topping in the pie pan. Sprinkle bacon and sausage over the egg mixture. Top with the remaining shredded cheese.

8. Ask an adult to bake the pizza for 35 to 40 minutes or until cheese is bubbly and golden brown.

9. Cool for 10 to 12 minutes before serving.

TIP:
To prevent oil splatters, blot off all water from the vegetables before adding to the hot skillet.

CREATIVE OPTION:
Substitute ¾ cup diced ham for the sausage.

For a heartier version, eliminate the sautéed vegetables. Double the cheese, triple the bacon, and add two eggs.

These dreamy, creamy spreads are perfect for eating with bagels, on toast, or as fruit dip. The chocolate strawberry dip is my favorite!

CREAM CHEESY SPREAD BAR

PUMPKIN PIE SPREAD

INGREDIENTS:

8 ounces cream cheese, softened
¼ cup canned pumpkin
2 tablespoons brown or coconut sugar
1 tablespoon maple syrup
1 teaspoon cinnamon
2 teaspoons pumpkin pie spice
1 teaspoon vanilla extract
¼ cup chopped pecans or walnuts

SPECIAL TOOLS:

electric mixer
blender

INSTRUCTIONS:

1. With an adult's help, use the electric mixer to blend cream cheese in a mixing bowl until light and fluffy.

2. Mix pumpkin, sugar, maple syrup, cinnamon, pumpkin pie spice, and vanilla extract with an electric mixer on medium—low speed until blended.

3. Use a spoon or spatula to stir in the chopped nuts.

4. Transfer mixture to a small serving bowl or plate. Cover and refrigerate for at least 1 hour before serving.

CREATIVE OPTION:
For a nut-free version, substitute shelled pumpkin or
sunflower seeds for the chopped pecans or walnuts.

continued next page

CHOCOLATE STRAWBERRY CHEESY SPREAD

INGREDIENTS:

1 cup fresh strawberries, hulled and diced
¼ cup honey
1 teaspoon almond extract
½ teaspoon cinnamon
¼ cup unsweetened cocoa powder
8 ounces cream cheese, softened

INSTRUCTIONS:

1. Place half of the strawberries in a blender, and puree. Add the honey, almond extract, cinnamon, and cocoa powder. With an adult's help, mix on medium—low speed until blended.

2. Add the cream cheese. Blend on medium until smooth and creamy.

3. Transfer the mixture into a small serving bowl. Gently stir in the remaining strawberries and mix until combined.

4. Cover and refrigerate for at least 1 hour before serving.

TIP:
If your strawberries are very sweet, reduce the honey. If they're more tart, add a little honey.

CREATIVE OPTION:
Instead of adding the cocoa powder, reduce the honey to 2 tablespoons. Then mix in ¼ cup miniature chocolate chips.

For a fruity Kylie Jean Strawberry Spread, skip the chocolate. Mix strawberries, almond or vanilla extract, and 1 tablespoon of honey into the whipped cream cheese.

VEGGIE DELIGHT SPREAD

INGREDIENTS:

3 green onions, finely sliced
½ carrot, peeled and diced
½ stalk celery, diced
¼ cup diced red, orange, yellow, or green pepper
3 tablespoons parsley, finely chopped
½ teaspoon garlic, minced
2 tablespoons fresh or dried dill
1 pinch black pepper
8 ounces cream cheese, softened

INSTRUCTIONS:

1. Mix the fresh vegetables, parsley, garlic, dill, and black pepper together.

2. Add the cream cheese. With an adult's help, blend with an electric mixer on medium until smooth and creamy.

3. Transfer mixture to a small serving bowl or plate. Cover and refrigerate for at least 1 hour before serving.

CREATIVE OPTION:

Make your veggie dip savory. Add 1/4 cup each of crumbled, cooked bacon and grated cheddar cheese. Add a little kick with half a 4.5-ounce (127.6 gram) can of roasted, diced green chili peppers.

These pastry twists are fancy! Momma will love them. I could make these for her on Mother's Day with a smoothie on the side.

FRUITY PASTRY TWISTS

FRUIT FILLING:
½ cup fresh or frozen peaches, strawberries, or apples
1 teaspoon honey
¼ teaspoon vanilla extract
1 tablespoon cinnamon

CREAM CHEESE GLAZE:
½ cup cream cheese, softened
5 tablespoons milk
1 teaspoon vanilla extract
1 tablespoon butter, softened
1/3 cup powdered sugar

TWISTS:
1 package frozen puff pastry sheets
2 tablespoons butter, melted
2 tablespoons sugar
½ teaspoon cinnamon

SPECIAL TOOLS:
blender
silicone baking mat or parchment paper
pizza cutter
basting or pastry brush

INSTRUCTIONS:

1. Remove pastry sheets from packaging. Carefully unfold and separate 8 sheets. Cover with plastic wrap and let them thaw at room temperature for 30 minutes, or in the refrigerator for 4 hours. Then shape them into eight rectangles.

2. Ask an adult to preheat oven to 375 degrees.

4. Toss the frozen fruit in a blender. With an adult's help, puree the fruit. Combine the pureed fruit with honey, vanilla, and cinnamon in a bowl.

5. Line a baking sheet with a silicone mat or parchment paper.

6. Spread the puree mixture on four of the puffed pastry rectangles. Then place another rectangle on top. Press them together, and crimp the edges with a fork.

7. Use a pizza cutter to cut the rectangles into strips. Press and crimp edges. Twist each strip three times. Brush with melted butter.

8. Mix the sugar and cinnamon together. Sprinkle over the top of each twist.

9. Carefully place the strips on the baking pan. Have an adult place the pan in the oven and ask them to check on the twists after 8 minutes. Bake for 2 more minutes, or until golden brown. Remove from oven and cool.

10. With an adult's help, beat cream cheese, milk, vanilla extract, and butter in a small bowl with an electric mixer until smooth. Slowly add the powdered sugar. Beat on medium until the texture is creamy. Drizzle glaze over each twist.

CREATIVE OPTION:
Mix up the fillings! Jams, applesauce, lemon curd, or pie filling taste great too. Savory fillings, such as cream cheese spreads, give them a different flavor. Create mozzarella and basil twists by using tomato paste, shredded mozzarella, fresh basil, and oregano.

TIP:
Remove only the number of puff pastry sheets you plan on using right away. Wrap unused sheets in plastic wrap. Place them back in the box, tape it shut, and return to the freezer.

Crisp and sweet, these Open Faced Apple 'Wiches are easy to make and easy to eat!
Sometimes I sneak a bite or two to Ugly Brother. He likes them too!

OPEN-FACED APPLE 'WICHES

INGREDIENTS:
one large apple
nut butter of your choice

SPECIAL TOOLS:
parchment paper

TOPPING SUGGESTIONS:
thinly sliced bananas or strawberries
shredded coconut
dried cranberries
granola
shelled sunflower or pumpkin seeds

INSTRUCTIONS:

1. Wash the apple thoroughly.

2. Have an adult slice the apple crosswise into four thick slices. Carefully cut out the center core.

3. Pat each slice dry with a paper towel.

4. Scoop 1 tablespoon of nut butter onto an apple slice. Cut a piece of parchment paper about the same size of the apple. Press the parchment paper over the apple to spread the nut butter to the edges.

5. Remove the parchment paper. Set aside for the next apple slice.

6. Sprinkle toppings of your choice onto the apple.

7. Repeat steps 4 through 6 with the rest of the slices.

TIP:
To make nut-free apple 'wiches, use sunflower or coconut butter instead.

CREATIVE OPTION:
Use your favorite nut butter, or try a new one! Peanut, almond, hazelnut, and tahini are all yummy choices.

I know y'all have a favorite pup, and you know I do too! Ugly Brother's going to love these delicious doggie treats. They give him the sweetest doggie breath. I'm glad, because he gives lots of kisses!

UGLY BROTHER'S SWEET BREATH BAGELS

INGREDIENTS:

4 tablespoons coconut oil

⅔ cup water

1 egg, beaten

¼ cup fresh chopped peppermint leaves (or 1 tablespoon dried)

½ cup fresh minced parsley (or 2 tablespoons dried)

2 cups whole wheat flour

¼ cup wheat germ

SPECIAL TOOLS:

cooking spray

donut cutter, or large and small round cookie cutters

INSTRUCTIONS:

1. Ask an adult to preheat oven to 350 degrees.

2. Lightly coat a baking sheet with cooking spray.

3. Mix the oil, water, egg, peppermint, and parsley in a small bowl. Set aside.

4. Combine the flour and wheat germ in a medium bowl. Add the wet mixture and mix well.

5. Place the dough on a floured surface and roll it to ¼—inch (1.3—cm) thick. Cut out bagel shapes with the donut cutter.

6. Repeat step 5, gathering the remaining dough into a ball and re—rolling.

7. Place the bagels 1 inch (2.5 cm) apart on the baking sheet. With an adult's help, bake for 35 to 40 minutes, until lightly browned.

8. Have an adult remove the baking sheet from the oven. Cool the bagels on a wire rack before feeding them to your favorite Ugly Brother.

TIP:
Store the treats refrigerated in an airtight container for up to 3 weeks, or in the freezer for up to 3 months.

Makes 15 to 18 treats

Read More

Archer, Joe, and Caroline Craig. *Plant, Cook, Eat!: A Children's Cookbook.* Watertown, Mass.: Charlesbrige Publishing, 2018.

Chandler, Jenny. *Great Foods for Kids: Delicious Recipes and Fabulous Facts to Turn You into a Kitchen Whiz.* Weldon, Owen, Spi Edition, 2017.

Peschke, Marci, Marne Ventura, and Mary Meinking. *Kylie Jean Craft Queen.* North Mankato, Minn.: Picture Window Books, 2014.

Internet Sites

Use Facthound to find Internet sites related to this book.

Visit *www.facthound.com*

Just type in 9781515828501 and go!

 Check out projects, games and lots more at **www.capstonekids.com**

Books in this series: